D0505873

PLANNING, DOING AND REVIEWING

Related titles of interest:

Baby and Toddler Development Made Real
Sandy Green (1-84312-033-X)

Essential Skills for Managers of Child-Centred Settings
Emma Isles-Buck and Shelly Newstead (1-84312-034-8)

Planning an Appropriate Curriculum for the Under Fives
Rosemary Rodger (1-85346-912-2)

Planning Children's Play and Learning in the Foundation Stage
Jane Drake (1-85346-752-9)

Other titles in the same series:

Self-development for Early Years Managers
Chris Ashman and Sandy Green (1-84312-197-2)

Managing People and Teams
Chris Ashman and Sandy Green (1-84312-198-0)

Managing Environment and Resources
Chris Ashman and Sandy Green (1-84312-200-6)

PLANNING, DOING AND REVIEWING

Chris Ashman and Sandy Green

Illustrations by Dawn Vince

David Fulton Publishers

David Fulton Publishers Ltd
The Chiswick Centre, 414 Chiswick High Road, London W4 5TF

www.fultonpublishers.co.uk

First published in Great Britain in 2005 by David Fulton Publishers
10 9 8 7 6 5 4 3 2 1

Note: The right of the authors to be identified as the authors of this work
has been asserted by them in accordance with the Copyright, Designs and
Patents Act 1988.

David Fulton Publishers is a division of Granada Learning Limited, part of ITV
plc.

Copyright © Chris Ashman and Sandy Green 2005

British Library Cataloguing in Publication Data
A catalogue record for this book is available from the British Library.

ISBN 1 84312 199 9

All rights reserved. No part of this publication may be reproduced, stored in
a retrieval system or transmitted, in any form or by any means, electronic,
mechanical, photocopying, or otherwise, without the prior permission of the
publishers.

Typeset by Mark Heslington, Northallerton, North Yorkshire
Printed and bound in Great Britain

CONTENTS

ACKNOWLEDGEMENTS

Gina has, as always, supported me to keep going – a crucial element to any successful plan is the encouragement of important people who care.

Continued guidance and support from co-author Sandy, along with effective monitoring of my progress has also been proof positive of a team approach to implementing any plan.

My work in further education and with the College nursery at Norton Radstock has provided many opportunities to explore, improve upon, discard, suffer and use a variety of required or desired planning approaches. The conversations with Pete Skinner have helped me to further my understanding of linking planning with action and improvement.

Chris Ashman

As always it has been a pleasure to work with Chris, supporting his writing throughout the series. My husband John continues to have an important role to play, showing interest and offering useful ideas. My own understanding of professional management has been directly influenced through working with Chris in the past, and I thank him for the opportunity to re-explore these processes during the development of this series.

Sandy Green

Chapter 1

FOUNDATIONS FOR PLANNING

This chapter covers:

- Harnessing the power of having clear values
- The benefits to planning of knowing your customers' needs
- Linking what you say you will do with what you actually do
- How having a plan will help even when facing new situations

JUST IMAGINE

Let your imagination wander. Think of the perfect Early Years service.

What does it look like? Can you see the faces of the children … and the staff? Are there any smells that gently touch your senses and add to this state of perfection? What noises and levels of noise do you hear? Can you picture yourself in the setting, what does it feel like?

BECAUSE YOU ARE WORTH IT – WHY BOTHER TO MAKE PLANS?

The title of this section 'Because you are worth it – Why bother to make plans?' could be viewed as putting the answer before the question. The imaginary perfect service that you were invited to create and explore may not be achievable within present circumstances. However, with good planning and enough people believing in the same (or a similar) vision it will be more possible in the future.

Because you and the children and the staff are worth it, is why you as the manager of an Early Years service bother to make plans. These plans will encompass day-to-day tasks and activities. They will also paint a picture of how the service will change and develop over the next few years. Because you are worth it is the starting-point.

Because you are worth it you will take the time and effort to plan a service to meet or even exceed the needs of parents, children and staff.

Because you are worth it you will bother to make plans, even though you know they will have to change in the future.

Plans help us to do a better job.

SCENARIO CASE STUDY

'It's out of date as soon as it's printed!' declared Sonia. If it weren't for the inspectors, she thought, there would be less need for writing any plans for her Early Years service. Perhaps all that was needed was a 'things to do' list, good job descriptions and team meetings. 'Then we could all get on with working with the children.'

Everywhere you turn in the world of Early Years you are made aware of a need for planning. The need to plan the curriculum and activities for children is well accepted by all practitioners, but a manager's need to plan for the future of the service may be less well accepted or understood.

As a manager you will find yourself in positions where you need to persuade people with the sense of your argument, lead people with the conviction of your belief, and justify action with a weight of evidence.

The process of planning can help you achieve all these. It can also help you to arrive at the correct course of action for your service by testing your own perception of what is going on. Planning also provides you with a focus on predicting the future.

The world of Early Years provision is as dynamic as any other sector of commerce or industry, in the private or public sector. In many situations you, as the Early Years manager, may be balancing pressures including:

❑ public sector accountability
❑ demonstrating the meeting of standards
❑ providing good value care and education
❑ projecting future demands and occupancy rates
❑ financial or investment predictions.

It's not what you say you do, it's the way that you do it

ACTIVITY 1.1

Ask yourself the question 'What does my service exist for?'

Note some of your ideas. Try to think of at least five.

_____

_____

_____

_____

_____

Comment

You may have generated a whole range of ideas about the purpose of your service. These could include – 'We exist to ...

❑ provide great childcare and education
❑ support parents with affordable and secure childcare
❑ make a profit (surplus) to enable us to continue providing a service
❑ make sure young children get the right start in life

❏ help prepare children and parents for school experiences.'

The list you generated may be similar to some of these or demonstrate very different and unique thoughts.

Completing this activity should help you consider the fundamental purpose of your service and help you start to identify some of the important values that you hold about the provision offered.

STARTING-POINTS

You can already demonstrate the skills of a planner. As an experienced Early Years practitioner you are able to:

❏ Identify aims
❏ Set objectives or goals
❏ Consider resources required
❏ Create activities to achieve goals
❏ Review progress
❏ Evaluate outcomes.

As a manager, however, it is worth spending time to consider the impact of your plans upon the practice of other people. Being effective and efficient are important for any manager. Being a manager in Early Years you will want the plan to be more than that – to be the **best way** of doing something.

SCENARIO CASE STUDY

'We need to get ready for the Ofsted visit next month,' Sheila reminded her team. 'The Inspector will be looking at how much we have improved on our policies and procedures, as we were only just OK last time.'

'Don't worry Sheila I'll get that sorted. I've found this really useful website that I can download all the policy statements that you could want. Each one has an easy to follow procedure. Some even have methods for monitoring the effectiveness of the practice – with examples,' enthused Robin.

'Mmm, tempting in some ways. But that isn't really the way we do things, is it?' questioned the worried manager.

ACTIVITY 1.2

Write down at least three reasons why Robin, in this scenario, might not be suggesting a good idea.

_____

_____

_____

Value your values

Before the planning starts, at any level, you have to have the foundations in place.

In terms of planning for the future of your Early Years service the foundations are your agreed values.

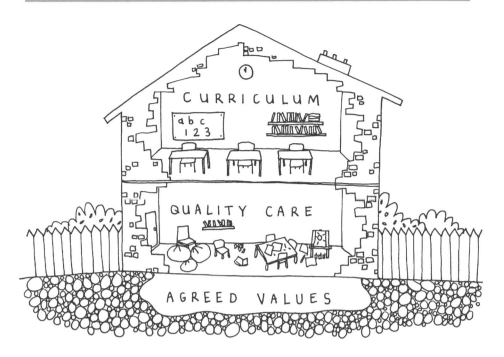

Once you are clear about these and have expressed them within your team and to parents and children, they become a framework in which to plan and operate. They also help you deal with situations that you have not predicted or events not planned.

There are many different ways that you can go about identifying your service's values.

ACTIVITY 1.3

Imagine you are leading an activity to create a statement of your service's values. This statement should clearly set out to other people what you put at the centre of your approach to Early Years provision and management.

Write down some alternative activities that you can think of to achieve this.

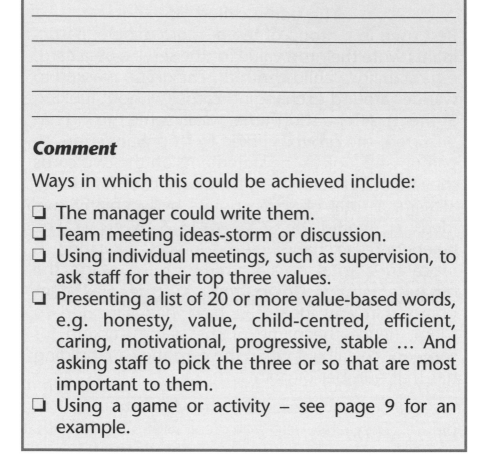

_____

_____

_____

_____

_____

Comment

Ways in which this could be achieved include:

- ❑ The manager could write them.
- ❑ Team meeting ideas-storm or discussion.
- ❑ Using individual meetings, such as supervision, to ask staff for their top three values.
- ❑ Presenting a list of 20 or more value-based words, e.g. honesty, value, child-centred, efficient, caring, motivational, progressive, stable ... And asking staff to pick the three or so that are most important to them.
- ❑ Using a game or activity – see page 9 for an example.

How you go about such a task will communicate some different values about 'how we do things around here'. For example, if you favour the method driven by the manager you will send out messages about a very different set of values compared to those based upon more inclusive approaches.

So it really is not _just_ what you say you do, it is the way that you do it.

The game called '35'*

Best used in a group of ten or more people, participants write their top value for the service on a card,
e.g. 'stability', 'child-centred'. The group is asked to
wander around exchanging cards (without looking
at them). After a short time, when some mixing has
occurred, the group is asked to stop wandering, to
pair up and look at the statements on the two cards
they hold. Between them they have two minutes to
allocate a total of seven points between the two
ideas (it could be 7–0, 6–1, 5–2 etc.). The
wandering, exchanging and points allocation is
repeated a total of five times. At this stage the
organiser counts down from 35 (the maximum
points that any ideas can have had allocated to
them, hence the name of the game), asking for
someone to call out when the card they are holding
has that number of points.

Tell the world

Once you have a clearly agreed set of values you need
to consider them. Are they ones that you and other
significant people can agree with and commit to? If
enough of your team can genuinely accept them as
their own (terms like 'buy in to them' or 'own them' are
often used) you need to communicate these to the
world ... or at least those parts of the world that may
be interested. People such as parents and carers,
potential new staff (as part of the recruitment process)
and Inspectors will be quite obvious audiences for this
information. In addition you may want suppliers, neighbours or other Early Years providers to know about your

---

* Taken from the work of Dr Sivasailam Thiagarajan (see p. 17)

TAKE CARE THAT YOUR ACTIONS DON'T CONTRADICT YOUR STATED VALUES

foundation values. This will form an important part of your marketing and publicity activities.

By sharing with others these identified values you will also have made a public commitment to them. In this way you will now have to act in ways that reflect these values, or people will notice.

UNCHARTERED TERRITORY

SCENARIO CASE STUDY

'The crew were getting worried,' Daphne declared. All the children were listening with full attention to the story of the explorers on board The Good Ship Nellydo. 'It had been nine days without fresh water and the biscuits had run out. Captain Ted was getting confused.

"Head West" she ordered. "And make it lively. No, cancel that and head South." "Make your mind up, please!" cried Rag Doll. "I don't know what to do. I've never been here before," exclaimed the Captain. "Any ideas, crew?"'

'What would you do?' asked Daphne to the pre-school group. 'Ask my Mum,' said Simon.

When 'Mum' doesn't know

As a manager you will not always have the luxury of drawing upon your own experience or even that of someone more experienced. Sometimes it will be the case that you have a great plan, but that reality turns out differently from how you thought it would.

When you are faced with a new situation you need to decide what to do. In such cases the set of values that

WHEN MUM DOESN'T KNOW

you have agreed can provide you with a reassuring foundation upon which to base your decision and actions.

SCENARIO CASE STUDY

'Honesty, Caring and Good Listening' stated the sign on the walls of Butterfly Pre-School Service.

Janet, the manager, glanced at the words as she heard one of the parents repeat, 'I think that my handbag has been stolen.'

What was Janet to do?

ACTIVITY 1.4

Think about this scenario. If you were Janet, what are your options? Don't just note down the first course of action that you think of, create at least three alternatives.

_____

_____

_____

_____

_____

_____

Comment

One useful approach to planning is to review your options. So the discipline of creating alternatives is good practice for later. If you were Janet, the ideas you have generated could then be checked against the values of Butterfly's.

One course of action could be to say to the parent, 'Go and look through all the places that you may have left it, then ask the staff if they have seen your handbag.' How would this check out against the values of the service? Does it demonstrate the commitment to Honesty, Caring or Good Listening? Subtleties such as tone of voice and body language will carry weight along with the words spoken and context or environment. The point is that having the values stated should act as a framework for decisions to be made in new situations – it will act as a standard against which all actions are measured.

WHAT MAKES YOUR SERVICE DIFFERENT, SPECIAL OR UNIQUE

A good manager develops empathy for the point of view of other people. Try putting yourself in the position of one of your customers. If you were a parent or carer of a young child, why would you choose your team and service to care for your child – why is it better for you and your child than the setting down the road?

You may arrive at a whole range of factors that could be important to parents or carers. Ideas might include:

❏ Excellent care and education
❏ Caring and professional staff
❏ Convenience – times of opening or close to home or work

❏ Cost and value for money
❏ Flexibility
❏ Stimulating environment.

When adults choose your service they consider alternatives open to them for the care of their child. These might involve decisions about their own availability (work or care), family members looking after their child, or other professional Early Years carers (childminders, crèche, nursery, pre-school) could be options. The school that their child may attend as well as the reputation of your service and others in the area that they hear from other parents will also carry weight.

If you were to rank honestly the factors you have identified in some order of importance, from the perspective of parents, what would be top?

It might be useful to consider how and why this might differ from your own ranking.

Depending upon what you have selected you may feel comfortable, even proud of the factor – e.g. excellent care and education – or perhaps a little disappointed – e.g. convenient to home.

The point of exploring this within the planning process is similar to the consideration of values addressed earlier. If you know what customers currently appreciate about your service you can choose to plan to maintain that or develop other factors over the next phase of planning and change. If parents choose you because of the quality of your care then plan to ensure it remains the best around. If they opt for you because you are convenient then build upon that advantage, adding other quality factors to the experience of both the parents and their child.

Some managers may believe that they are in a position where they do not have to consider any other Early Years provision as competition. This may be because of lack of alternative services for the numbers of children seeking care, or because currently the opposition is way behind in quality, inspection reports, equipment, staff or any other of the important attributes of a great service.

Plans are about preparing for the future. Just because you are secure in the current market and situation this cannot be relied upon to predict the future. What if a large organisation set up in competition locally, or key staff leave or an inspection goes badly? If these factors do not seem likely in your situation then the continued development of the care and education of the children should be a big enough driver to plan for improvement.

Learn from history

Do you remember when your money, held in your bank account, was only available to you between 9.30am and 3.30pm Mondays to Fridays. Even then you had to queue at the counters, especially in the lunchtime when fewer cashiers were on duty (taking their lunch breaks). In these 'old days' up until the late 1980s, the high street banks saw no reason to change or improve. They had enough customers, so much so that they had lines of them waiting for a service! Once some new ideas – telephone banking, then cash machines, then internet banking – were introduced, change was forced upon these more complacent providers. They had to change very fast (with accompanying pain) to stay in business.

Learn from the banks! Even if you see no need to plan for improvement and change, it doesn't mean there is no need – just that you don't see it ... yet.

REVIEW OF – FOUNDATIONS FOR PLANNING

This chapter has helped you if you can

- ✓ Describe why the values that an organisation holds need to be acted out through their planning process.
- ✓ Outline the importance of knowing your customers and the importance of this in your planning process.

References and suggested further reading

K. Blanchard and T. Waghorn (1997) *Mission Possible*, McGraw-Hill.

N. Kline (1999) *Time to Think*, Ward Lock.

H. Koontz and H. Weihrich (1988) *Management*, 9th edn, McGraw-Hill.

Websites

www.thiagi.com This website promotes the work of Dr Sivasailam Thiagarajan (known as Thiagi). He invents and shares ideas for games and activities that help learning and development. A great man and a great site.

Chapter 2

LEADING FROM THE FRONT

This chapter covers:

- The manager's responsibility to take a lead
- The usefulness of your organisation's agreed values
- A 'Why and How' to having an organisational mission and vision

---

SCENARIO CASE STUDY

'They've done it again!' sighed Juliet. 'No! I don't believe it,' comforted Isabel. 'Oh yeah, I asked my team to tell me who, of the three of them who had requested it, should have next week as annual leave and they couldn't decide.'

'Wouldn't decide, more like it. I thought you said your empowering approach meant the team took more of these routine decisions and left you to make the big ones, Juliet.'

'What a mess! Now Muggins will have to be the bad guy again.'

THINK AND ACT AS A LEADER

Whether your management empire is a small team or a large organisation, other people will look to you for leadership.

This responsibility came with the job role. If there is a difficult or unpopular decision to be made others will look towards you. While many may offer their ideas, or even regale you with hindsight-empowered wisdom of what you should have done, few team members will volunteer to take the tough decision and be seen to act as the leader.

Nor should they. You are the manager.

Accepting the responsibility to lead is the first step. Knowing what to do to demonstrate such leadership involves a more complex, but fulfilling and useful set of actions.

When the time comes for planning for the future, your role as a manager is a key role to success. This does not mean however that the task of planning is the sole responsibility of the person called manager.

There are different ways to go about leading others. Some situations may call for a 'rallying cry' approach and leading from the front. Other skills can be applied to facilitate team members with the right skills and confidence to take a lead. Your skill as a manager is to choose appropriate styles for the situation.

At different times your team will need you to guide, prompt, challenge and inspire. One of the most important attributes to develop as a manager will be that of being a clear thinker.

SCENARIO CASE STUDY

'So we know many things about sheep now.' stated Bernadette. 'Does any one know anything different?' she let the question hang in the air as the Pre-School group started to think about lunchtime.

'I know something different!' shouted Mandy with excitement. 'My Dad told me that there are two sorts of shepherd. One sort stands behind the herd of sheep and with the dogs drives them forward. The second sort walks in front and the sheep follow.'

'Now that is interesting. Why do they follow?' asked Bernadette.

'Because they trust the shepherd, Dad says,' replied Mandy.

ACTIVITY 2.1

Think about a situation you have experienced where a successful plan has been made. It could be work-related or personal – the example you might use could be something like planning for a key worker review meeting, a Christmas party or wedding, or a holiday or home move.

What factors made the plan successful?

_____

_____

_____

_____

Comment

You have probably identified a whole range of things, including:

- ❏ Having a clear goal or target
- ❏ Identifying and gathering required resources
- ❏ Communicating with other key people to let them know what help you needed
- ❏ Listening to the views of others who had an interest in the outcome
- ❏ Having a written version of the plan to help you review progress over time
- ❏ Someone to help you keep motivated or focused when the going got tough
- ❏ Others who understood or believed in the planned action who could help you as part of a team approach

Many of these factors need other people to make them work. You can also do many things on your own. As a busy manager it may feel like it is sometimes quicker to do things yourself, but you really know that such a view is shortsighted. As managers we need other people.

The best plans are shared ideas and approaches to action that work towards a common goal.

Sharing takes time

In the same way as you work with young children to help them explore ways of sharing, to discover the frustrations and benefits of being part of a group, you may need to remind yourself of the benefits of sharing the process of planning.

SCENARIO CASE STUDY

Chris was really pleased with herself. It had taken a long time, but surely been worth the effort. 'We have needed a new fire drill in case of fire, or other emergency,' Chris announced at the team meeting. 'Here is a draft I have written for your thoughts and comments.' Chris knew of the importance of including the team in decision-making and had carefully chosen the words to encourage participation. After all, Chris thought, this is such an improvement on what we had before I expect to receive some praise for its clarity.

'Any suggestion for improvement?' Chris asked after a couple of minutes reading time for the rest of the team.

'Well, have you thought about how we would cope if it were lunchtime, with fewer staff?' asked Tamsin. 'I think it's good as far as it goes,' added Berni; 'But I'm not sure what to do to help our children with mobility disabilities.'

'Oh blow!' thought Chris. 'I just wanted you to say how good it was, not try to improve upon it!'

'Time to listen and share ideas for a better plan,' said Chris's internal reflective voice.

It is often quicker to create a plan yourself. You can generate ideas and options, dismiss unrealistic or crazy approaches instantly, and avoid being sidetracked by some irrelevant line of thinking.

Such an approach may be quicker, and in some circumstances it may be appropriate, such as in an emergency.

SOMETIMES, BEING CONSULTATIVE IS LESS EFFECTIVE!

Emergencies, hopefully, don't happen every day. In many Early Years situations the plan can be developed over a reasonable period of time. It can therefore involve more people. While this will take more time it should result in the end in a more accepted and successful plan.

CHANGING VALUES INTO ACTION PLANS

Successful planning

If you believe anyone can write a good plan you need to consider what makes some plans more successful than others.

We have already considered the extent to which other people should be involved in forming the plan. This is a key factor, but not the only one.

The test of any plan is the action that follows. There are some fundamental questions to keep in mind when planning and implementing any plan. These include:

❏ Do people know what is expected of them?
❏ Do team members carry out their part of the plan?
❏ Who can amend the plan in light of changing circumstances?
❏ What do team members do if they face a situation not predicted within the plan?

The work that you and your team will have done on identifying and communicating the core values of your Early Years service are key to positive answers to these questions.

Values as a planning framework

If your values are based upon inclusive approaches and continually working at effective communication you will be off to a sound start.

SCENARIO CASE STUDY

'What does the policy say?' asked Libby. She was feeling uncomfortable about this request for extra leave from the new practitioner. Paul had only been working here for three months and was asking for time off to attend a five-day conference for which he would pay the fees.

'Our CPD policy doesn't really cover this request,' replied Trish. Libby thought things through. 'Right then, let's check back against the Service Values Statement of "… investing to develop the best in staff, while ensuring we provide an excellent service to children and parents". Does that help us to decide?'

Having a clear values statement can help you as a manager to make a decision when you have no previous reference point and the policy statements don't cover the situation. By consideration of any tensions within the context of your values you also provide the means to explain to others the reasoning behind the decision.

SCENARIO CASE STUDY

'You must be gutted, Paul. That conference would have been so interesting,' commiserated Jenny when she heard that his request for leave to attend had been turned down.

'I am disappointed, for sure, but the way that Libby explained it I understand that the first priority is to make sure the children have an excellent service. It's what we say in our Values Statement, isn't it? With other staff already booked off on leave, it wouldn't be fair. Trish mentioned that if I could swap leave with someone else it might be possible. Aren't you on leave that week?'

VISION AND MISSION

The first concrete planning statements for an organisation or team to put in place are about its Vision and Mission. These set out the purpose for the organisation's existence.

Definitions

There are many ways of defining such statements. Simple definitions that work for most managers would be:

Vision Statement – an expression of the 'big picture' for the service, which includes reference to the values believed in.

Example: *Through a child-centred approach and value of diversity we will contribute to our thriving community.*

Mission – a statement of the long-term aim of the service.

Example: *To be the best provider of an Early Years service from birth to Pre-School in the county.*

It is not worth getting too worried about the similarities or differences between vision and mission (or indeed values) statements.

The point of them is to:

❏ Help you to clearly communicate why your service exists
❏ Enable you to communicate effectively – to customers and the community externally, and internally with staff and other managers
❏ Provide you with the broad planning framework to support other plans, e.g. curriculum, staffing, resources, finance.

HOW TO CREATE A STATEMENT

As well as a way of clarifying an organisation's purpose, the advantage of creating statements can be that they provide a great opportunity to bring the team together. Statements about values, vision or mission that result from team approaches will be better accepted and used by the whole team. They will also have helped to develop the team, as they will create challenges to overcome, differences to understand, options to choose from, and similarities to recognise.

Team Day

A time for the team to be together, but away from the normal working environment and the care of the children, can be invaluable. It may be that creating such a time seems unrealistic. You may, for example, believe that you cannot afford the time for all staff to be 'at work' but no income being generated.

Check such assumptions carefully. There may be some period during the year that occupancy is usually significantly lower than normal. The 'lost income' from being closed for staff training would be less then. Alternatively, you may be able to make arrangements with other services to provide relief staff to allow some of your team to have time together. Be creative!

After all that effort, you (or your line manager or the proprietor) will want to know what great benefits are to be gained from a team day.

ACTIVITY 2.2

Think about times when a team you know have had time to themselves, away from their usual responsibilities. Based upon your thinking identify a range of potential benefits that such time has provided the team

_____

_____

_____

Comment

Ideas you noted could include:

❑ Time to share ideas and perspectives of work with each other
❑ Opportunity to identify solutions to known problems, or improve practice
❑ Time to plan ahead for teams focused upon specific age ranges of children such as 0–3s 'Birth

> to Three Matters' or 3–5s 'Foundation Stage Curriculum'
> ❏ Training input for all staff on Child Protection, Equality of Opportunity, or service policy and procedure updates
> ❏ Share time out of normal roles – get to know each other as people with different interests as well as team members in Early Years provision.

Whatever you want to use this precious time for needs to be planned well. If you use it to create statements that the team can agree on regarding values, vision or mission you need to make sure that the process is organised. There is nothing more frustrating than team members feeling that the day has been a waste.

To help you get the most out of the time, consider

❏ Clarifying your aims for the day, e.g. to create a team statement of shared values
❏ Alternatives for leading the day, e.g. you as the manager, another manager from the organisation, your mentor, a trainer or teacher from your local college
❏ Agreeing with the leader for your day what their brief is, e.g. to facilitate discussion so that everyone has an opportunity to contribute, or to keep the group focused upon achieving the task within the timescale
❏ Communicating to all participants practical arrangements and something of what to expect, e.g. 'Start time is 9am, finish at 4.30pm; bring contributions to shared picnic lunch. You will be encouraged to

explore new ways of thinking about our service for the future.'

There are many methods that you could choose to help your team create statements. An example is 'Pair and Share'. You ask your team to work in pairs to discuss and agree on key points that they want in the team's statement.

After a set time period ask two pairs to combine and share the ideas. They have to then create a new shared statement that all four people can agree upon.

The next stage is to repeat the combinations until the whole team has an agreed statement.

As with other types of activities, planning the day will pay off. You will also need to think about how you will evaluate the outcome. It will be useful to know what has been achieved, such as:

❏ Did you achieve your planned goal or goals?
❏ In what ways did participants value the time (or why didn't they value the time)?
❏ What has been agreed to be done as a result of the day – next steps?
❏ How much did it cost? – salaries, hire charges, refreshments, fees, lost income ...
❏ Was it worth it? – opinions of all participants of costs versus benefits.

Team meetings

As an alternative to one full day's concentrated time there are other benefits to spreading the process over a series of team meetings. These can be used for generating ideas, considering options and agreeing on shared outcomes over time.

Having space and time between different phases may actually improve the reflective consideration of alternatives and promote improved outcomes.

The danger is that a lack of focus and momentum will result in no agreed outcomes.

By being clear about how much time or how many team meetings will be devoted to creating statements of values, vision and/or mission a similar process can be followed.

Parental involvement

So far we have only explored this process with the involvement of staff. There can be great benefits from inviting parents into the process as well.

ACTIVITY 2.3

List as many ideas as you can that can be viewed as positive contributions resulting from involving parents in statement creation.

_____

_____

_____

ACTIVITY 2.4

Now list any limitations or potential concerns you might have about involving parents in this activity.

_____

_____

_____

Comment

Positive contributions that parents can make include:

❑ Their views as parents, customers of your service
❑ Outside perspective, with interest and commitment to the excellence of the service
❑ A focus upon every child as an individual
❑ They will want to know and expect to hear about future progress on agreed outcomes.

Concerns might include:

❑ They focus upon their needs and their child too much
❑ The presence of parents restricts the creativity of team members to explore new thinking
❑ Some parents may 'take over'
❑ Parents are only interested in the short term (while their child is cared for) and this is about the medium to long term
❑ You will be so concerned about the parents' involvement you won't focus upon the task.

Remember, the unique view of parents can bring fresh challenges and thinking to you and your team. Some form of inclusion in the process – perhaps a separate parents' evening or other form of consultative activity like a questionnaire – will produce positives for your service.

Community involvement

You may view yourselves as contributors to your local community. Many Early Years providers acknowledge their place as supporters of local parents and their efforts to improve the experience of children and parents. This could be a great opportunity to involve community representatives in your service. It also means more than holding car boot sales or summer fayres.

Listening to what local people think of your service and what they expect or hope for in the future can be extremely valuable to you as a manager.

You could try inviting local people into some consultative meetings. Perhaps a more informal gathering would be better. Either way you need to be clear about the sorts of questions you would like their views about.

Ideas could include:

❏ What do you think about
    The opening hours of the service?
    The quality of care?
    The facilities and our impact upon the local environment?
    The curriculum provided?
    The effectiveness of our communication with parents and carers?

❏ What should we do in the future to improve
   Our service?
   Our value for money?
   Our community support?
   Our image in the locality?
   Our links with other organisations, e.g. schools,
   health services?

Children too

Wow! Having thought about involving staff, parents and community representatives in your large-scale planning, you didn't think it ended there, did you?

   The danger with creating statements about values, visions or missions is that any consensus decision by a committee may produce a set of words that is either bland or meaninglessly confusing to others who have not been part of the process.

SCENARIO CASE STUDY

'Great! We've done it. Well done everyone,' declared Evangeline. 'So our new mission statement is "Daisy Chain Nursery will seek to aim to provide very good quality care, education and challenge (within a safe and secure environment) to many local children between the ages of 6 weeks and pre-school. Our commitment to developing staff is second only to our focus upon the child as an individual with all their diverse and unique qualities and potential."'

'Mmm,' Reflected Olivia. 'Perhaps it needs a bit more work on it.'

'Yes,' quipped Jamie, 'I don't think we've mentioned equality of opportunity yet!'

It would be fascinating to set up a listening activity with children. Ask them to tell you what they believe is the purpose of your service. Out of the mouths of your children may come the best statement of values, vision or mission you could find.

SCENARIO CASE STUDY

A new manager overhears a conversation, between two pre-schoolers. They have been asked why they think they come to nursery.

'My dad says that I come to nursery to learn my colours and how to kick a ball properly,' said Freddy.

'I am learning about other people and how to be nice, my mummy says,' replied Alfie.

'What do the babies learn do you fink?' asked Freddy.

'Well, to be happy and smiley, even when their mummies are at work,' said Alfie, 'And to look at toys and books.'

'Do they read the books, do you fink?' asked Freddy.

'Nah, they learn by looking at the pictures,' stated Alfie emphatically. 'And they copy actions. I knows that, 'cos it's what I still do and I'm bigger than them babies.'

Snippets of interaction like this may provide you with a glimpse of how children like Freddy and Alfie are demonstrating their learning under different aspects of the Foundation Stage Curriculum. In this simple exchange of conversation can be seen elements of the aims of all six aspects of the Foundation Stage, together with reference to the ethos of the Birth to Three Matters strategy.

REVIEW OF – LEADING FROM THE FRONT

This chapter has helped you if you can

- ✓ Describe how you would plan to review (or create) Vision and Mission statements for your team.
- ✓ Outline the positives and negatives for your service of involving all managers, staff, parents, community and children in creating your Vision and Mission statements.

References and suggested further reading

K. Blanchard and M. O'Connor (1997) *Managing by Values*, Berrett-Koehler.

M. Fullan (2004) *Education in Motion: Leading in a Culture of Change* (Workshop Tour May 2004 handbook).

Websites

www.michaelfullan.ca

Chapter 3

MAKING PLANS

This chapter covers:

- An overview of how management plans fit together
- Explanation of strategic planning as a process
- Exploration of strategic planning and creative thinking

YOU ALREADY KNOW HOW TO PLAN

Plans are all about having ways of doing things that can be used to remind yourself and others of actions to take over a period of time.

Your organisation will be required to have plans in the form of policy statements and procedures for all kinds of things.

We have confirmed that as an Early Years practitioner you will be used to planning, for example activities for the children, preparation for events or planning your own continuous professional development (CPD).

As a manager the law will require you to have plans regarding health & safety and risk assessments. You will also become involved in a whole range of other sorts of planning.

Before considering a management approach to strategic planning in some depth it is useful to think about how various plans link together. After all there should be some coherence between the different sorts of plans used within your setting.

A HIERARCHY OF PLANS – HOW DIFFERENT PLANS LINK TOGETHER

A really useful way of understanding how different plans relate to each other has been described by Harold Koontz and Heinz Weihrich (1988, pp. 61–9). In Figure 3.1 you can see that the purpose or mission statement is placed at the top of the pyramid. That mission acts as the overall plan that all other layers of planning contribute towards.

The building blocks described rise from the foundations of budgets through to the glue of procedures and rules. Upon these rest the key organisational objects.

In brief terms, each layer is defined in these ways:

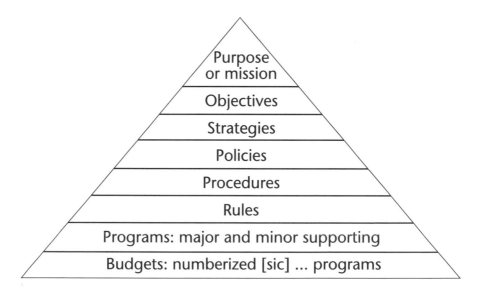

Figure 3.1 The Hierarchy of Plans (Koontz and Weihrich, p. 62)

Budgets 'statements of expected results expressed in numerical terms'

Programmes 'a complex of goals, policies, procedures, rules ... to carry out a given course of action'

Rules '... specific required action or non-action, allowing no discretion'

Procedures '... guides to action ... chronological sequences of required action'

Policies 'general statements or understandings which guide or channel thinking in decision-making'

Strategies have the purpose to '... determine and communicate, through a system of major objectives and policies, a picture of what kind of enterprise is envisioned'

Objectives are the 'ends toward which activity is aimed'

Missions are required, making the organisation 'meaningful'
          (from Koontz and Weihrich 1988, pp. 61–9)

Such definitions, taken from general management theory, can be applied to Early Years activities that include the responsibilities of both practitioners and managers.

Budgets set out what resources are needed and the costs involved (or income expected) related to your Early Years service.

Programmes explain complicated approaches to issues that might arise. An example could be the action that results from a Child Protection case conference. Plans need to include complex sets of actions to be combined and coordinated.

Rules explain some of the things that just have to be done in the right way. Examples could include financial decisions, such as issuing receipts to parents for payments due; or that information-handling, like the medical data relating to a child, is kept secure but accessible to key staff.

Procedures need to be written to explain to staff how to carry out routine or occasional tasks such as risk assessments, emergency evacuation drills, care and control of medicines or how to run a keyworker case study.

Policies are statements used to provide staff with an overview about the principle to use in dealing with such issues as equality of opportunity, child protection, administration of medication, or sharing information with parents and other adults.

Strategies could set out how staff are expected to provide a holistic range of care and education for children as individuals. This strategy would draw upon a collection of the policies and procedures in place within the service.

Objectives at an organisational level would be the big targets for the year, such as 'to increase occupancy rates to 89% minimum average' or 'expand provision to cover 7am to 7pm availability from Mondays to Fridays'.

Mission is the grand purpose of the organisation for existing, such as, 'To be the best Early Years provider in town' or 'To provide excellent value for money in a child-centred environment'.

We have explored the idea that planning should not be seen as an isolated or individual process. Therefore any explanation of how various plans fit together – a hierarchy – needs to be placed within a context.

SCENARIO CASE STUDY

'What are we going to do?' asked Diane. She had become increasingly frustrated with the frequent breakdown in the staff rota that meant she had to cover for absent colleagues.

'I know what you mean,' jumped in Rashid. 'We need to plan a strategic response to the "Birth to Three Matters" agenda.'

'What?' the rest of the team said together.

Sometimes you will need to plan for a specific short-term issue. At other times a long-term, broad-based approach is required.

STRATEGIC PLANNING

In management, 'strategy' is one of the most used examples of jargon. You, of course, know what it means.

> Strategies have the purpose to '... determine and communicate, through a system of major objectives and policies, a picture of what kind of enterprise is envisioned'

So, a strategic plan is a document that sets out, usually over three or more years, the way ahead for the organisation and its service.

A strategic planning framework

A strategic plan is usually an overarching document that sets out the major developments and changes envisioned over the next few years. It includes:

A Scene-setting
B An understanding of the service's current position in the market
C Identified changes that could affect future developments
D The main aims for the future development of the service or business.

The following short guide will help you explore what lies behind these headings and act as a guide to help you if you are required to write a strategic plan.

A. Scene-setting

This provides a description of the working context of your service. Things that could be included are factors such as:

❑ *Who are your customers?*
Factors to be considered are as follows: the number of families that you help; the numbers of their children and their age groups; the range of social and economic backgrounds of those families; the age ranges of the parents; the ethnic groups repre-sented; whether the parents are in full-time or part-time employment.

❑ *Who are your competitors?*
Within a competitive distance – what is the number of alternative providers that exist; what major strengths do these competitors have?

❑ *Other factors that affect your area*
Community features may be an influence upon your service. These could include the degree of, and types of, employment opportunities; local work patterns (shift work or usual office hours); the reputation of the local schools; the use of local services or out-of-town resources.

ACTIVITY 3.1

Using the headings above, make some brief notes to set the scene for an Early Years service that you know.

Customers

Competitors

Community

Comment

You may well have found one or two of these headings more difficult to describe. It might be that you really do not know enough about the *scene* to describe it. If that is the case, that's great! You have identified something that will be useful to learn more about in the future. Knowing about the environment your service operates within is important for planning to improve.

B. *The service's current market position*

❏ *What is the size of your share of the local market?*
   It will be useful to estimate how many children in the age ranges that your service includes use Early Years provision within the local area. When you have identified this you can estimate how big a percentage you have of the overall market. It will also be interesting to estimate the share taken by each of your main competitors.

❏ *What does your service's internal market look like?*
Within your service there may be 'hot spots' or low-demand areas – maybe to do with age groups, e.g. a waiting list for babies not yet born.

❏ *What are your current Strengths and Weaknesses?*
You can use the Ofsted inspection framework, or the NVQ Early Years units as a framework to consider current areas of strength and weakness.

ACTIVITY 3.2

Reflecting upon your service's current Strengths and Weaknesses is a useful habit to practise. Think about an Early Years service you know well and identify the top five Strengths and five most important Weaknesses (or things to improve) it currently has.

Strengths	Weaknesses

Comment

Review your lists and consider these questions:

Do you think that a survey of parents would find broad agreement about most of these areas you have identified?

Would the lists change if you considered things from the viewpoint of the children, your staff team, Ofsted, or a competitor service?

C. Changes that could affect future developments
These are useful to predict when creating a strategic plan. The former sections are based upon your interpretation of what already exists. This heading asks you to dream (or have nightmares) about the future.

❏ *What **social** changes are likely to have an impact upon your service?*
Changes to the make-up of your local population or work style patterns might be considered, e.g. a new housing estate or the closing of a factory, along with anything that could influence attitudes to the use of Early Years provision.

❏ *Are there any new ways of doing things, resulting from changes in **technology**, which could have an impact upon your business?*
In the past decades the big technological changes that have affected provision and need for professional childcare have included: relatively cheaper private transport making the distance between home and provision less of an issue for many; mobile phone ownership resulting in the perception of easier and quicker verbal communication between parents and practitioners; improved medical intervention for premature-born babies or children with disabilities resulting in a widened range of care needs being presented.

❏ *Will there be **economic** changes that impact upon parents or your service?*
The willingness and ability to pay for Early Years provision is linked to parents' economic situations. This is affected by taxation, income and

employment, the benefits system, local fees structures, demand for places and the supply of provision. Other factors could be home prices that affect your staff as well as parents.

❏ *Can you predict any trends to local, national or international **politics** that may play a part in your future?*
As well as national government policy this might include local planning applications for community facilities, employment or home-building. This section also asks you to consider changes to the law – specifically connected to Early Years provision or generally to employment and health & safety.

The STEP grid
To identify changes that could affect future developments of your service you can use the STEP approach (sometimes known as PEST).
   STEP is a mnemonic that stands for

❏ **Social**
❏ **Technical**
❏ **Economic**
❏ **Political**

Against each of these headings you would identify potential change that may have an impact upon your service. An easy way of recording this analysis is to construct a grid.

SOCIAL	TECHNICAL
ECONOMIC	POLITICAL

The SWOT grid

The next stage of strategic planning is to consider how the environment in which you operate has an impact upon the service that you provide.

Together with your ideas from STEP you can now complete a process known by another mnemonic of SWOT that stands for

- **S**trengths
- **W**eaknesses
- **O**pportunities
- **T**hreats

Strengths and Weaknesses are to do with things that are inside your control, the service provided. Opportunities and Threats are associated with the STEP analysis and relate to how the external world may have an impact upon your service in the future. A complete SWOT grid could look like this:

STRENGTHS
Many excellent staff.
Financially secure.
Great parental support.
	WEAKNESSES
	Some poor performing staff.
	Policies and procedures
	   need reviewing to fully
	   comply with recent
	   legislation.

OPPORTUNITIES
New housing development
   could increase demand.
	THREATS
	Main local employer
	   threatened mass redun-
	   dancies.
	Planning permission
	   received for extending
	   premises of a close Early
	   Years competitor.

ACTIVITY 3.3

Go back and review your outcomes from completing activities 3.1 and 3.2. You could complete the STEP grid for an environment you are familiar with. You can link these to a service you know well to construct a SWOT grid. Write down the major items that appear to fit under these headings below.

STRENGTHS	WEAKNESSES
OPPORTUNITIES	THREATS

Comment

Your SWOT analysis will of course be unique to your service and environment. The level of detail does not have to be great. The purpose is to record the main points as a result of considering the environmental context and the internal position of the Early Years service.

D. The main aims for the future development of the service

You are now in a position to consider what your grand aims for the future could be. This will be based upon the understanding, predictions and analysis already completed.

Four themes of Service, People, Information and Resources taken from the NVQ Management framework may help you.

Using the theme of service as an example, the strategic plan will need to consider what, if any, changes need to be identified for your service to develop, grow and thrive in the future. Having completed this exercise using the service theme you could try it while your focus is on people (staff), information (marketing, publicity and internal communication systems) and resources (finance and budgets, equipment, capital and buildings, and the environment in which you operate).

Service as an example

You may need to extend, alter or improve the service offered to parents. This area may also get you thinking about the day-to-day experience of the children. Questions to explore may include:

❏ Do we provide what parents need?
❏ Could we develop a service that parents would want – perhaps something that they haven't even asked for yet?
❏ What is the experience like for the different age ranges of children we work with?
❏ Is our preparation for their progress into the next phase of the curriculum or moving on to school as good as it could be?

You should add more of your own questions to explore the future possibilities further. Your staff team could help as well.

Management Health Warning
– Don't get stuck in a rut

Someone once warned me, 'Choose your rut carefully. You'll be stuck in it for a long time!'

Such pessimistic thinking has no place here. You and others need to think creatively, even a little crazily, about how the future could be.

Remember those high street banks of the 1970s? They didn't believe that they had to change. Their customers had accepted queues at lunchtime for years. It was only when someone (crazy?) started putting cash into machines in the wall and setting up 24-hour telephone banking that the slower thinkers realised their customers liked what was offered, even though they had not asked for it.

ACTIVITY 3.4

This is your chance to let loose your imagination and dream a little. From the viewpoint of parents or children describe the most fantastic Early Years service of five years' time. What does it provide? Where? How? What extras can you invent that would make this service so special that parents and children would write letters and send emails to their friends, relatives and the press or television?

Write down some of your ideas, or draw diagrams

and pictures to illustrate some of this creative thinking.

_____

_____

_____

_____

_____

_____

Comment

There are no right or wrong ideas. However, the next stage for a good strategic plan is to consider which of these ideas represents the direction that the service should move towards.

Choosing the best ideas for your strategic direction

Some of the ideas that you have generated will be more successful to implement than others. Unfortunately none of us actually knows which are the best ideas. This is an exercise in creating the future.

As a manager you have to be brave enough to make decisions that shape change. You will use skills of planning, analysis, budgeting, judgement, balance and creativity. You may also be lucky!

To improve your luck, this quick checklist of tests can be used to assess each idea for future direction: Is it …

❑ Realistic?
❑ Feasible?
❑ Affordable?
❑ Acceptable?

For a strategic idea, each heading is used to check out how the idea measures up.

Is it realistic to achieve or a flight of fancy? Checks could include technical or legal boundaries.

Is it feasible to achieve or too complicated and outside of the realm of any changes that could be made to resources or environment, for example?

Is it affordable or able to be resourced? This may well mean changes to the availability of current financial or capital assets, but this check asks for a prudent approach to be taken to your creative ideas.

Is it acceptable to the range of stakeholders that would need to support it to happen? This test can be added to by asking whether the change would be desirable? Viewpoints such as parents, children, politicians and regulators, staff, the local community and neighbours need to be considered.

SCENARIO CASE STUDY

'That's great work, team!' said Rachel. The creative thinking and research of the past few weeks had culminated in a set of interesting and inspiring strategic aims.

'Now we need to assess the ideas we have generated to identify the ones we choose as the Strategic Aims for the next five years.' added Helen.

The first idea they considered was, 'Extend our opening hours to provide a service from 7am to 9pm Monday to Friday and 7am to 6pm Saturday and Sunday.'

Using the four-point checklist the team worked in groups, each taking one area to test the idea. After half an hour the team shared their conclusions.

Realistic – OK as long as kept within legal framework. It doesn't rely on any technology changes.

Feasible – OK as long as issues of staff rotas, keeping track on attendance, and other practical factors were organised effectively.

Affordable – OK as no extra capital costs. It would need more income to generate funds for extra staffing, running costs, marketing and publicity to stimulate use.

Acceptable – Parents would like the flexibility. Shift work employees would benefit. Staff would need to be recruited or existing staff hours renegotiated. Salaries may need to reflect 'unsocial hours'. Ofsted and LEA views uncertain. Neighbours may object to any interruption from early morning or evening use. Break-even points for occupancy need to be worked out.

'Well, that has provided more food for thought,' reflected Rachel. Then she challenged the team: 'We need to consider whether the questions and the constraints around "acceptability" outweigh the overall benefits of keeping this development within our new Strategic Plan.'

Strategic planning made simple

By following the approach outlined in this chapter you will be able to create a strategic plan for your area of responsibility, for any aspect of your provision or for the whole service.

The process is the same, however far removed the factors involved in your specific situation. Remember that predicting the future is never easy, but it is made the more difficult if you are confused where you are in the present.

The techniques of the STEP and SWOT analysis provide you with a clear structure to use in discussions with others.

You will then end up with a good enough understanding of where you are in the present, and where you plan to be in the next few years.

Watch out for the danger signs
There are some dangers it would be good to prepare for when planning strategically with others. Here are a few to be aware of.

Analysis paralysis – This is the need for some people to research even more, or explore things one more time to more fully understand the present situation. Avoid this by setting time limits on the stage of gathering facts and opinions. You can also remind people that this is not an exact science, it is about a 'good enough' understanding.

Un-checked Blue Sky Thinkers – Having people with vision to dream future improvements is great, even necessary. However, many dusty strategic plans exist that have unrealistic and over-ambitious aims. The danger is that the aim is so far away from the present reality, no-one has the energy to make steps in that direction. Think big, but commit to a stretching aim.

Declaring success too early – It is very tempting to view the creation of your strategic plan to be a completed task. You have consulted, researched, listened, generated ideas, STEPed and SWOTed, now you have the written-up plan. The hard work now begins to use the strategic aims to inform your actions and keep the strategic plan alive through your day-to-day work.

REVIEW OF – MAKING PLANS

This chapter has helped you if you can

✓ Describe the various levels of planning within an organisation and make links between them to show how they support each other.
✓ Complete a STEP description of the working environment your Early Years service is operating within.
✓ Undertake a SWOT analysis that links the internal strengths and weaknesses of your service with the external opportunities or threats.

References and suggested further reading

K. Blanchard, P. Zigarmi and D. Zigarmi (1990) *Leadership and the One Minute Manager*, Fontana.

H. Koontz and H. Weihrich (1988) *Management*, 9th edn, McGraw-Hill.

T. Peters and A. Austin (1985) *A Passion for Excellence*, 5th edn, Fontana.

Websites

www.dilbert.com/comics/dilbert   is an excellent site for light relief from the earnest endeavour of creating a meaningful mission statement

Chapter 4

PLANNING FOR QUALITY

This chapter covers:

- Links between a strategic plan and actions
- Ways of knowing if change is happening
- Small or large-scale improvements to quality

KNOWING YOUR AIM IS JUST THE START

SCENARIO CASE STUDY

'It was the longest journey that Jenny and Ahmed had ever taken,' read Jasmin to the listening group of children. After pausing slightly to check that all her group were still involved and content to carry on, she returned to the text. '"Where are we going?" asked Ahmed. "Are we there yet?" questioned Jenny, adding, "How will we know when we've arrived?"'

The strategic plan is only part of the planning process. It is a very important part of managing successfully. To work without having a clear idea about how you want to change and develop things in the next few years often means events overtake the manager and their service. Instead of having a *big plan* for the future to keep checking progress against, a manager will start reacting more to other immediate factors.

What to do with the strategic aims

Having spent time and energy in developing a set of strategic aims that set out the direction for your service you will want to start working towards achieving them.

This may seem an obvious statement. However, too often the requirement to construct a strategic plan is not followed up sufficiently with the links to shorter-term operational plans and action. When this link is missing some managers and staff still seem surprised when, clearing out the cupboards in a few years' time, they find the 'old strategic plan,' flick through it and wonder why 'nothing really changed'.

Remember change won't happen by just writing a strategic plan.

Things have to be made to happen by taking action.

OPERATIONAL PLANNING AND ACTION

You already know about planning for action. You are an experienced Early Years practitioner who can plan and implement plans.

The term operational plan is used to mean a method for managers to map out the things that need to be done, in a particular order over a specified timescale, to achieve a defined objective.

Sometimes the term 'action plan' is also used. Each

organisation will have its own understanding of what is meant by these terms (or indeed invent its own terms). What is important to keep in mind is that there is one overall big plan for setting the aims and direction. This needs short-term specific plans to make sure that things get done.

As a manager you will need to commit operational plans to record. These operational plans are the links between strategic aims and practical implementation.

For each strategic aim you need to consider the operational activities that will be required to move from

---

ACTIVITY 4.1

When you write a plan what headings do you use to help you?

_____

_____

_____

Comment

Many people would use headings such as:

- ❑ **Aim**
- ❑ **Objectives** or goals
- ❑ **Method** or actions
- ❑ **Resources** required
- ❑ Who is **responsible** to carry out the action?
- ❑ When is the action due to be **completed**?
- ❑ How will you measure the **quality** of what has been completed?
- ❑ How will you **review and evaluate** your learning?

where the service is to closer to where it is described within the strategic plan. The operational plan will cover a shorter timescale than the strategic aim it is developing – perhaps six months or one year. It will be written in enough detail for those responsible for its implementation to be able to follow it. The operational plan will also be resourced and funded to support its achievement within the time planned.

SCENARIO CASE STUDY

'How will we know when we've arrived?' echoed Daddy. *'What a good question, Jenny. Mum, can you show the children the photograph of our holiday home? I'll go and get the travel tickets.'*

'Please take the list so that you get the other things we need.' Mum reminded Dad.

The children looked at the glossy brochure and imagined themselves splashing in that pool, running on the beach and eating at the cafes it showed.

'Right then,' said Mum. *'Dad's out getting the tickets and shopping we need. Lets check whether we have done our jobs.'*

'Yes,' shouted Ahmed, *'Who's got the plan? There's only three days to go and there's so much to do. I've still got to pack Mr Ted.'*

There are many ways to record an operational plan. The example in Figure 4.1 may help you decide upon a style that suits you and your service.

Name of the organisation:				
Strategic aim this plan develops:				
Objective: Overall responsibility for the objective is held by:				
Actions/method	Resources	Who	When	Quality measures
Final review and evaluation				

Figure 4.1

WHAT GETS MEASURED, GETS DONE

At the end of the process of planning comes the really important point of it all – doing it!

A clearly formed and well-communicated operational plan should ensure that everyone who needs to, knows the actions for which they are held responsible. The resources required are clearly identified. The timescale to complete the tasks is set.

Measures to assure quality together with methods of checking progress are vital to the successful implementation of any plan.

ACTIVITY 4.2

How many ways can you think of to check that a plan is being put into action?

_____

_____

_____

Comment

Ideas that you may have identified could include:

❑ **Observation.** Can you see things happening?
❑ **Review meetings.** With those responsible for the agreed action.
❑ **Progress reports.** Verbal reports to project meetings or written updates.
❑ **Set up a steering group.** With a number of important operational plans being implemented simultaneously it might be good to have a separate steering group to review progress on all plans.

'Everyone was working so hard, but we weren't getting far'

There will be many ways that could be used to check on progress. These methods can also help identify blocks to success early on, with enough time to do something about them. In addition, frequent checks provide a great chance to reconsider and, if required, update the plan. On occasion these progress reviews might help you to realise that the plan is no longer the best way of achieving your desired objective.

Monitoring progress towards the outcome is different from seeing if people are working hard. Sometimes it appears that progress must be being made because everyone is working so hard. This may be a false view. The approaches you use should help you to decide objectively whether appropriate progress is being

SCENARIO CASE STUDY

'Wow, those shops were busy,' said Dad as he returned carrying armfuls of bags. 'Now I'm running late.'

'Did you get everything?' enquired Mum.

'Pretty much, I think, and you'll be pleased with the 3-for-2 bargains of bumper-pack sun cream I found. That should last us for years!' said Dad proudly.

'Can I see the tickets, Dad?' asked Jenny.

'What tickets are those, darling?' said Dad. Jenny, Ahmed and Mum just looked at Dad in silence.

made. If it is not then you have to investigate 'Why?' Then you start to put things right.

It will be an important part of your role as the manager to demonstrate that the actions involved in this operational plan matter to other people. They are not something to do when things are quiet. They are important developments that others in the team will be relying upon.

LITTLE STEPS OR GIANT LEAPS

There have been some great management thinkers who have described processes of continuous improvement. People such as W. Edwards Deming (Kennedy 1991, pp. 36–40) identified the need to have process involved in working practice that looked for improved ways of doing things. This greatly influenced post-war rebuilding of the economy in Japan, and the subsequent growth and economic strength of Japan towards the end of the twentieth century has been attributed to this approach. Later, from the 1980s, management influencers like Tom Peters (Kennedy 1991, pp. 125–32) have challenged managers from all sectors not only to help staff to make things a little better, but to make huge changes to how things are done.

Both approaches are demanding improvement from the way we work and provide an Early Years service. Both are really telling us that 'just because your service is popular and successful now, doesn't mean it will be next year'.

SCENARIO CASE STUDY

Two Early Years providers ('Butterflies' and 'Poppies') are close enough to each other to be competitors.

Both services are popular, enjoy good levels of occupancy, have an annual financial surplus and feel secure for the future.

One day an announcement is made public that the largest local employer is relocating to a different part of the country. Employees will be offered relocation or redundancy. The local press predicts a large increase in unemployment as no other similar-scale investment is expected.

The management teams of both 'Butterflies' and 'Poppies' are updating their strategic plans.

'Butterflies' knows that 48% of the children it provides a service for have one or both parents employed directly by the affected employer. Staff and managers estimate a further 25–35% are closely connected via family members.

'Poppies' management also know that many families have parents working for this employer.

The 'Butterflies' team have been working on improvements to their policies and practice, they were keen to develop the scope of provision by extending opening hours. They had also started negotiations with the employer about some provision at their site for employees.

At 'Poppies' the management had a view that keeping on doing what they were proven to be good at was the best approach. They did not consider expansion. It was more in line with their thinking that things just needed to be fine-tuned.

As the manager of your service you will be faced with a decision to either improve what you do to make it better – more effective or efficient, or meeting increasing wants or needs of customers – or to change what you do altogether.

Your judgement in this will be unique to you and your situation. By applying a structured approach to planning – basing actions on your understanding of the environment you work in and your current strengths – you will be a more effective manager.

Whether or not your plans are implemented exactly as you intended will depend more on factors outside of your control than on your own skills and determination. However, being a well planned manager, with actions grounded in shared and appreciated values and belief, you will be better equipped and supported than many other managers.

Remember that, as in most activities that involve a mixture of skills, experience and luck, the more you do something the 'luckier' other people think you are.

Be lucky.

REVIEW OF – PLANNING FOR QUALITY

This chapter has helped you if you can

✓ Ask more questions than you have answers for about your Early Years service – in terms of the quality, strengths, things that need to improve, ideas for new ways of doing things.
✓ Feel brave enough to raise this agenda of improvement (small steps) with your team and organisation.
✓ Be confident enough to involve other people in *dreaming for the future* about the best Early Years service of five years' time.

REFERENCES AND SUGGESTED FURTHER READING

C. Kennedy (1991) *Guide to the Management Gurus*, Century.
K. Blanchard and T. Waghorn (1997) *Mission Possible*, McGraw Hill.

Website

www.tompetersnew.com

A STRATEGIC PLANNING MODEL

This model may help you set out a planning document. Feel free to copy it, add to it or alter it in any way that helps you.

Scene setting

Customers
(*description of the range of existing customers using the provision*)

Competitors
(*outline of the range of competitors that our provision has – including main strengths or weaknesses*)

Community
(*description of the main characteristics of the community we serve*)

Current market position

> **Market Share**
> (*estimate the current share we have of the actual local market*)

> **Internal Market**
> (*description of the existing segments of the market we serve – including busy and quiet areas*)

Strengths and weaknesses

Use the two boxes in the SWOT grid to record these.

STRENGTHS	WEAKNESSES

Environment and future

Use the STEP grid

SOCIAL	TECHNICAL
ECONOMIC	POLITICAL

Future and aims

Bring forward the Strengths and Weaknesses information into the full SWOT grid. Consider Opportunities and Threats in relation to the STEP analysis.

STRENGTHS	WEAKNESSES
OPPORTUNITIES	THREATS

Strategic aims

Once you have identified the opportunities and strengths, or any threats and weaknesses, you can decide upon the strategic aims for your provision. These need to be set out to describe what you aim to achieve over the next few years. It is these aims that need to be reviewed in light of progress made at regular intervals over the period of the strategic plan.

Action plans can be drawn up to address each strategic aim using a pro-forma like this.

Action Plan

Name of the organisation:				
Strategic aim this plan develops:				
Objective: Overall responsibility for the objective is held by:				
Actions/method	Resources	Who	When	Quality measures
Final review and evaluation				

INDEX